let's play
I SPY
animals!

let's play books by
© Little Moon Joy Co

are you ready to play i spy?

the letters are not in alphabetical order, just like a real game of i spy.

i spy with my little eye, something beginning with...

C is for... camel!

d is for... dog!

i spy with my little eye, something beginning with...

a is for... alligator!

i spy with my little eye, something beginning with...

b is for...
bee!

i spy with my little eye, something beginning with...

e is for...
elephant!

i spy with my little eye, something beginning with...

g is for... giraffe!

F is for... fish!

i spy with my little eye, something beginning with...

h is for... hedgehog!

i spy with my little
eye, something beginning with...

L is for... ladybug!

i spy with my little eye, something beginning with...

j

j is for...
Jellyfish!

i spy with my little eye, something beginning with... K

K is for... kangaroo!

i spy with my little eye, something beginning with...

P is for...
parrot!

i spy with my little eye, something beginning with...

O is for...
OCTOPUS!

i spy with my little eye, something beginning with...

S is for... sheep!

i spy with my little eye, something beginning with...

M

M is for... monkey!

i spy with my little eye, something beginning with...

W

W is for... WOLF!

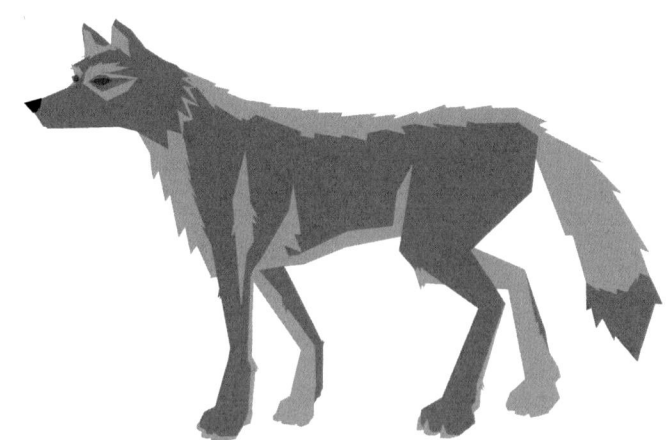

i spy with my little eye, something beginning with...

t is for...
tiger!

i spy with my little eye, something beginning with...

r is for...

rabbit!

i spy with my little eye, something beginning with...

Z

Z is for... zebra

Made in the USA
Middletown, DE
27 June 2020